A WORD WITH BEDE

PREVIOUS BOOKS BY NEIL CURRY

Poetry
The Plain People
Between Root and Sky
The Maidenhair Tree
Ships in Bottles
Walking to Santiago
The Road to the Gunpowder House
Other Rooms (Selected Poems)
Some Letters Never Sent
On Keeping Company With Mrs Woolf
A Northumbrian Book of Hours
Things Being Various

Translations
Euripides, The Bacchae
Euripides, The Trojan Women
Euripides, The Helen
Homer, The Bending of the Bow
Jules Supervielle, The Fable of the World
The Dream of the Rood

Criticism
Norman Nicholson
Christopher Smart
George Herbert (co-written with Natasha Curry)
Alexander Pope
Six Eighteenth-century Poets
William Cowper: a Revaluation
William Shenstone: Landscape Gardener and Poet
Samual Johnson: Writer
Horace Walpole

Topography
The Cumberland Coast

A WORD WITH BEDE

NEIL CURRY

All rights reserved. No part of this work covered by the copyright herein may be reproduced or used in any means – graphic, electronic, or mechanical, including copying, recording, taping, or information storage and retrieval systems – without written permission of the publisher.

Printed by imprintdigital
Upton Pyne, Exeter
www.digital.imprint.co.uk

Typesetting and cover design by The Book Typesetters
hello@thebooktypesetters.com
07422 598 168
www.thebooktypesetters.com

Published by Shoestring Press
19 Devonshire Avenue, Beeston, Nottingham, NG9 1BS
(0115) 925 1827
www.shoestringpress.co.uk

First published 2023
© Copyright: Neil Curry
© Cover illustration: St. Matthew, Lindisfarne Gospels (710–721)

The moral right of the author has been asserted.

ISBN 978-1-915553-10-2

ACKNOWLEDGEMENTS

Some of these poems appeared in the following publications:

Acumen, A Garland of Poems for Christmas, Scintilla, The London Grip, The Reader, TLS, Poetry Ireland, Wallace Stevens Review.

A Northumbrian Book of Hours and *Things Being Various* were first published as a Wayleave Pamphlets.

"It is the violence within which protects us from the violence without."

– Wallace Stevens

CONTENTS

Silence	1
Skellig Michael	2
The First of February	4
Abbot Ceolfrith Looks Back On The Plague	5
Ceolfrith and the Great Jarrow Bible	6
St. Cuthbert's Beads	7
St. Cuthbert and the Otters	8
Some Fragments from a History of Whitby	9
Wilfred and Hilda	11
from The Exeter Book of Riddles	12
Lindisfarne	13
And With a Feather	14
The Invasion of Lindisfarne	15
The Abbot Bids Farewell to his Builders	17
1812 – Overture and Closure	19
A Word With Bede	20
St Kilda	22
A Northumbrian Book of Hours	25
Things Being Various	31

SILENCE

Month after long winter month of numbing cold,
Then sandstorms, followed by a summer's heat
Such that one brush against a bare rock
Is enough to blister bare flesh; and never
A drop of rain, although snow lingers
Up in the gullies of the high peaks.
A god-forsaken hole you'd think.
Yet something in its emptiness,
The very aridity of the place,
Called to the Desert Fathers,
Determined to rid themselves
Of both pomp and prelate,
And discover the solace
To be found in time's
Twin antagonists:
Solitude and
Silence.

SKELLIG MICHAEL
for he hath founded it upon the seas

I

There being no desert
In Ireland where they might
Emulate St Anthony,
Fionán and his brother monks,
Twelve of them,
Set sail for the Skellig Rocks.

Eight miles off the coast
Of Kerry, their sharp stacks,
Like two hands raised in prayer,
And soaring sheer out of the waters
Of the grey North Atlantic.

Even landing there today, backed
By a flask of coffee, a BLT baguette
And (well, just in case) a cagoule,
There is no escaping that stairway –
Six hundred and seventy hand-hewn,
And hand-hefted slabs of rock –
Twisting and winding up a hillside
From whence cometh no help.

And then, at the summit: *the achieve
Of, the mastery of…*their monastery:
Six dry-stone beehive huts.

Such hardship – let alone attacks
By Vikings – would seem beyond
Endurance: the cold and the wet; a diet
Of fish and wind-dried seabirds; and yet,

And yet – matins celebrated by starlight,
And compline to the going down of the sun…

And as they drift into the dusk,
The Skelligs, garlanded by gulls,
Look to reach out once more
To Fionán and a remembered prayer

THE FIRST OF FEBRUARY

Presented with a *Calendar of Saints*,
Which of us would not go (page 32)
Straightaway to find out (the first of February)
Who among them (Ah, St Brigid) had been
Assigned to intercede for us this day?

Brigid of Kildare, that Irish country girl
Who turned water (bless her) into beer;
The patroness – if that's the word – of crafts,
And hearths, of poetry and things new-born.

And today, new-born lambs there are, jumping,
As ever, over small hills that are not there.
And no, that's not another fall of snow,
Simply the petals of a wind-blown blackthorn
Settling into the wet ruts of the lane.
Snowdrops too of course – *Eve's Tears* – their hoods
"Prettily edged about with green", as Gerard noticed.

Poised between the winter and the summer
Solstice, Celts this day would be celebrating
The Festival of Imbolc, when holy wells
Were to be attended to. Well, haven't we all
At some time tossed a coin – a small
One usually – into some fountain or other?

And then tomorrow, as well as Candlemas,
It's Groundhog Day, and with blue skies and longish
Spells of sunshine forecast. Never mind;
We've come through this far…

Keeper of the hearth, enkindle us;
Lady of the Lambs, watch over us.

ABBOT CEOLFRITH LOOKS BACK ON THE PLAGUE

Oddly enough, a mood swing
Was the first symptom: seemingly for no
Good reason a sense of anxiety was felt,
As though the body had some premonition
Of what was in store for it. Later came the
Fever; then a rash; the convulsions
And the bleeding; black apples
Growing in their armpits; flesh putrid.
And as for the stench…
                            Burials were a problem.
It's said of some they'd put up a good fight,
But there was no fight. You either
Died or you didn't.
                   It's funny the things
You bother about. What worried me most was what,
If I went, would happen to all the books
I'd brought back with me from Rome.
But I, as the saying goes, was *spared*. Just me,
And one small boy. Time passed, as it must.
We got by. Slowly put the place to rights.
Little as he was though, young Bede,
I doubt I could have coped without him.

CEOLFRITH AND THE GREAT JARROW BIBLE

In the suburbs of Sunderland…
    (No, that won't do.)
On land bestowed by Ecgfrith,
High King of Northumbria,
    (That's better.)
Were founded the twin-monasteries
Of Wearmouth and Jarrow,
Homes to Ceolfrith and Bede.

Ceolfrith, in whose scriptorium
Was penned the great Jarrow Bible.
    (You've never heard of it?)

Well, a thousand leaves of vellum,
And weighing in at over ninety pounds,
It was meant as a gift for the Pope,
But went missing for centuries
When Ceolfrith died en route to Rome.

Pampered now among the splendours
Of the Bibliotheca Laurenziana in Florence,
And catalogued as *Codex Amiatinus,*
It could be said to have come up in the world.

It would be nice though to think
It hadn't quite forgotten its roots;
That it's the same Jarrow Bible yet;
That those vellum leaves still hold
Some slight smell of the Tyne perhaps,
Some soft echoes of the clip-clop and burr
Of Abbot Ceolfrith's Geordie vowels.

ST. CUTHBERT'S BEADS

Here on my desk beside me is a silver
Cigarette box which once belonged
To my friend Michael, *aka* Br. Columba,
And inside it – no bigger than my little
Finger nail – two round green objects
That look almost like nuts or washers,
But are in fact fossils: segments
(And I quote) "of the stems of columnad
Crinoids" – creatures related to sea urchins
And starfish.
                   I found them, years ago
On Lindisfarne, among the slimy rocks
Surrounding Hobthrush, Cuthbert's Island;
And it's this has given them their other name,
Cuthbert's Beads, as it's said they were
Sometimes strung together to form a rosary;
(Not that anyone has ever found one)
Hours of searching brought me these two only,
And that's maybe why they're precious to me,
Or maybe it's because of where I found them,
Or their latency for prayer, or simply that
Being more than three hundred million years old
They form such a grand rebuff to impermanence.

ST. CUTHBERT AND THE OTTERS

*Down he went towards the beach
and out into the sea. At daybreak
he came out, knelt down and prayed.
Then two otters bounded out of the
water and tried to dry him on their fur.*
From: Bede's "Life of Cuthbert"

Reading Bede, we tend to think
It must have been guilt drove him to it,
His own sense of sin that sent him
Out into those waters, an act
Of penance, of contrition,
And self-inflicted too.
                          But what if
It was one of those nights
We sometimes have in late July
When it's really too hot to sleep,
And he'd stepped outside for a breath of air,
And then decided to wade about
In the waves for a while, and feel
The sand between his toes.
And what if there'd been a full moon
Above the silhouette of Bamburgh
And glints of phosphorescence,
And his prayers had been of thanks –
Thanks for the cool, soft breeze
And the sound of the waves
Dragging at the shingle; thanks too
That he'd been granted this great
Ocean at all, let alone a pair
Of lively little sea otters
To play about with?
                          And what if he was
Laughing, yes, and thinking of singing?

SOME FRAGMENTS FROM A HISTORY OF WHITBY

Those jet-black, black jet
Mourning brooches, so belovèd
Of Victorian thanatophiliacs,
Stemmed, of all things,
From the fossilized remains
Of giant Monkey-Puzzle Trees,
Vast swathes of which once swept
From here down as far as Kettleness.

And then there was Frank Meadow Sutcliffe,
Photographer extraordinary,
Whose lens caught those cheeky little
Curly-headed bobby-dazzlers
As they blossomed into fishwives.

And in 1768, a local lad, one James Cook,
Took command of the bark *Endeavour*,
A converted Whitby collier, looking
"Somewhat between a Dutchman's clog
And a coffin", and sailed for the Pacific
To observe *The Transit of Venus*. That done,
He opened his sealed orders:
"Now try and find New Zealand."

No. it did not bode well
That bruised and blood-red August sky,
And when Bram's storm broke
The *Demeter* was caught
Under full sail, foundered
Helpless, and reduced to splinters
In the very teeth of the harbour.

Then came the great Synod of Whitby,
St Wilfred arriving straight from Rome,
Resplendent, with his own personal army.
Cuthbert stayed silent. Little doubt
The way the votes would be going.

But let's not forget Caedmon,
Poor lad, cowering down in the cowshed
To get away from that voice
Which kept on pestering him to sing.
"Hwæt sceal ic singan?"
      Sing me
frumsceaft.
  "Hwæt?"
      ***Creation**,*
*Sing me the **Song** of my **Creation**.*
And he did.
   "Yes, by God, I did."

WILFRED AND HILDA

Leading lives of quiet desperation,
They were bound to meet up with each other
Somehow, Wilfred and Hilda. It's a
Comfortable, sensible-shoes sort of a name,
Hilda, isn't it? Likewise, Wilfred:
A man who keeps himself to himself;
Plays the odd game of bowls and reads the paper.
Not so in Whitby though, not when Hilda
Was abbess and ruled both houses, and not
In 664 when they called the Synod
(Caedmon was wise to keep out of the way)
And Wilfred, pomposity itself,
Arrived from Rome in all his splendour. Oh, yes,
He knew the date of Easter; he knew
When Christ had died, and why. Yes, and what's more,
Knew how to deal with pushy women;
How to pack Colman off to Iona again
And Cuthbert to Lindisfarne. The Church
Militant he would rid of all this Celtic guff.
Odd that he ended his days in a backwater
Like Oundle, where there isn't even a tomb.
His comeuppance? Maybe he's down there
Under those ugly new executive houses.
No, there's not a trace of either of them now:
Hilda and Wilfred, Wilfred and Hilda.

from THE EXETER BOOK OF RIDDLES

Some fiend fleeced and flayed me; robbed me
Of strength and life; sluiced me and steeped me
Time and again in ice-cold water; pegged me down
Under the sun till all my hair fell out.
Then came the pain of a knife's sharp edge
Scraping and biting into me. Later, after
Strong fingers had folded me, the feather
Of a bird brushed over my brown skin,
Leaving behind it tracks of dark marks,
Marks, so I'm told, mighty of meaning.
Strong men then bound me between boards;
Stretched yet more skin over me, and smiths
With wondrous skill clothed me in silver
 Embellished me with gold
To the greater glory of the Guardian of Hosts.
My name? Sacred the sound to all good men.

LINDISFARNE

All afternoon a cold east wind
Had parched the sand to a smooth, scraped vellum
The cursive run of the tide
Would scrawl across, stipple and etch.
Later when it had all but
Covered Cuddy's rock, dark cormorants
Hung out their wings to dry.

From his scriptorium window
Eadfrith sketched their great beaks and pebbled
Luxury of that beach. Now though
There was Jerome's *Prolegomena*
To be penned, 'Novum opus
Facere me cogis ex vteri…'
New work out of the old.

For such tasks, tired dexterities
Are never enough; echoes of echoes.
What's called for is that other gift
Which subverts logic with all
The nonchalance of nuance: a man
Conscious of the silence flooding his mind
And giving voice to it.

Whirlpools of ribboned interlace
He drew, maelstroms of colour: indigo
Verdigris, orpiment and woad;
Labyrinths and carpets of praise,
Of spirals, eyed-pelta and plait.
Craftsman, peacock and saint, Eadfrith's
Quills fluttered with the Word.

AND WITH A FEATHER

plant becomes fish
fish beast and beast bird
in this gorgeous zoomorphic
interlace of spiral and curve
branch feather and fin
interwoven in a celebration
of creation where we can see
plant become fish
fish beast and beast bird
in this gorgeous zoomorphic
interlace of spiral and curve
branch feather and fin
interwoven in a celebration
of creation where we can see
plant become fish

THE INVASION OF LINDISFARNE

Something's upset them.
The redshanks, as ever – with four or five
high-pitched shrieks and trills –
are the first to be up and off;
then it's the dunlin, knit tight
as a shoal of herring; flickerings
of white – aspen leaves in a high wind –
each time the flock dips and turns.

Did they see it, or sense it?
I've only this moment
myself made out what it is.

A peregrine, coming like a small black
anchor flung across the sky;
it slows,
rolls and climbs,
looking for some unlucky loner,
then stoops.

Locked onto its target it follows
every desperate lunge and dive,
answers every jink and sprint.
But it's no contest.
This is a Viking
got in among the monks,
the marriage of predator and prey.

One small puff of feathers and it's finished.

For a moment a few hang
in the empty air,
then drizzle down slowly
over the waves.

Something is dead…

                nor was it
thought possible that such
an inroad from the sea could be made.

Silence.

Then tentative
pitch-pipe sounds are heard.

The rest of us are still alive.

THE ABBOT BIDS FAREWELL TO HIS BUILDERS

They were leaving heathen as they'd come.
He had half hoped one might return
his part-wave, part-blessing.
It was still early of course,
and cowled in his long, black robe
he could, he supposed, have been taken
for another shadow and no thing of substance.

He would miss them – there was no doubt of that –
these masons, carpenters and quarrymen;
their womenfolk too – wives, they said,
whores, they were; he knew that much.

Not that it had ever been easy.
Those raucous songs they'd bawled out
in counterpoint against the Eucharist;
and that gargoyle – it had looked far too much
like poor old Brother Anselm to be funny.

Untouched they might have been
by what they'd done, but look
at what it was they'd done.

And there was something about their noisy
camaraderie he had it in himself to envy,
the fearlessness, their nonchalant
agility, even at the dizziest of heights.

The fluidity of things had always been
what most entranced him,
how, as the seasons came and went, each ring
of green wood toughened into heartwood.

Stone by stone,
amid a reek of beer
and onions that had outdone
whatever incense he might burn,
the abbey slowly had assumed its shape,
until, like that moment in an hour of prayer

when world and self cohere, the time had come
when every stitch of scaffolding was taken
down and there it stood, "prepared
as a bride adorned for her husband."
{Revelation, Chapter 21, Verse 2.}

There was no room for excuses any more.
Consummatum Est, he had half caught himself
thinking, and flinched. Light began to play
across the windows of the new scriptorium.

Yes, it was high time he faced up to the word.

1812 – OVERTURE AND CLOSURE

I

Tchaikovsky himself soon fell out of love
With it: the predictable boom of the big guns,
And those altogether-too-ecstatic bells.

Moscow burning, and the slow French trudge back
Through a frozen land was more the truth of it.
At 30 below they fought over fires.

Ate their horses. Some, looking up, glimpsed
A slight smudge on the night sky – the *Great Comet* –
Took it for an ill omen, and died standing.

II

May 25th. Jarrow. Nearly noon. Nothing
But broken cloud over Felling Pit. No comet.
It is one thousand and seventy-seven years

To the day since Bede died here, *borne aloft
By angels.* Below ground it's change-over time.
The earth mutters; first one seam then another

Explodes, sending dust and debris higher and
Higher, while ninety-two men, having no
Room to stand, are burned to death, mostly crouching.

·

A WORD WITH BEDE

"Hac sunt fossa Bedae venerabilis ossa"
(words over Bede's tomb in Durham Cathedral)

I've always liked that story of the monk
Carving your tombstone, and being at a loss
For words, well for an adjective at least,

To put in front of *bones* – so he left a gap,
And overnight an angel came and filled it in
With *venerabilis* – a name (it does now

Seem to be your name) that's really stuck.
There's something sort of *mildewed* though
About Venerable; it makes me think

Of *verdigris,* as if your Benedictine robe
Weren't always quite as fresh as it might have been,
And makes you seem perpetually old,

Which of course you weren't. Another story
Has it you were the little lad "nourished and taught"
By Ceolfrith, you and he the only survivors

When that Third Rider – plague – trampled down Jarrow.
Frightening for a child it must have been: those buboes
Big as apples, the retching and the deadly

Ring o' roses before the skin turned black.
Thanks be your own death was more gentle.
As you said: having lived without shame

You could die without fear. But managing
To hold on until you'd finished translating *John,*
That was a nice touch – those closing words of his:

"I suppose that even the world itself
Could not contain the books that should be written."
How many you yourself had written is something

I suppose we will never know. Alone
In your cell with your lampblack ink, and quills,
Recounting the exploits of the saints –

Their voyages, their miracles and derring-do,
There were times you doubted whether what you'd done
Had been enough, you who'd never ventured

Further than Lindisfarne, and that only once,
While so many of your friends had made their way
To Rome and back. But you were the maker.

Without you, we would never have known of the otters
That came running to dry Saint Cuthbert's feet
With their fur when he'd been praying in the sea;

Or of Edwin's thane likening our lives
To the flight of a sparrow – coming from
A howling winter's storm, into the light

And warmth of the mead hall, where great lords
Sat feasting, then straightway out into the storm again;
Or of the poet Caedmon who fled

From the song yet was found by the Singer.
Only books? Bede, hinny, you showed us miracles
Can flare out from so little as the turning of a page.

ST KILDA

I

The map the dominie had tacked up
On the schoolroom wall didn't even show
St Kilda, but then only a foreigner
Would have needed one to find his way past Mull
And Skye, and out through the Sound of Harris, then on
For fifty empty miles over the
Oily pitch and swell of the grey
North Atlantic.
                    Any St Kildans
Out of sight of land, with bad weather closing,
Knew they had only to watch the flight-paths
Of the birds: guillemot and gannet would wreck them
On the stacs round Borreray, while puffins
Scuttering back wave-high to Dun
Would prove a safe guide home to Hirta
And the Village Bay.

II

Birds. Or angels even
They must have seemed, the women
Plucking, in a cloud of feathers,
At the haul of fulmar their menfolk

Had themselves plucked off the cliffs
Of Conachair; cragsmen spidering
Thirty fathoms down, along the edges
Of guano, dependant on sheer faith

In their neighbours and on a horsehair rope,
Claim life those cliffs could, but always would
Sustain it while there were sea-birds
In such thousands to stew or dry;

Even a gannet's neck, turned inside out,
Made a snug boot, and oil from the fulmar
Not only fuelled their lamps, but was a panacea
For no matter what ills or ailments of the island.

III

Ultima Thule it was
Until the Victorians discovered it,
Sending in their missionaries
To pound out the parable

Of the Prodigal Son
To people who hadn't
Anywhere to stray to
And had never seen a pig.

Then steamers came, and summer visitors
With gimcrack charities and new disease,
Tipping the cragsmen with a penny each
To see the capering about on Conachair.

Pennies that the winter ferryman
Would finger from the eyelids of their dead.

IV

By lantern-light
They loaded a few more
Sticks of furniture
And the last of the sheep,
Then they drowned their dogs.

In the morning
According to custom,
In every empty house
There was a Bible left
Open at Exodus.

A NORTHUMBRIAN BOOK OF HOURS
i.m. Brother Columba, OSB
of Buckfast
Michael Kimber
(1944–2019)

1

During our dark absence, that trinity of killers, the bat, the badger and the screech-owl held sway, slew the sleeping and the unwary; now at starfade comes a regime-change; tentative at first, but then knuckling down to its key watchwords: *beholden* and *accountable*.

2

Through bog and heather, past village and hovel, Aidan had, at the King's command, walked from Iona to Bamburgh, but then, to a still further call, crossed over the sands to Lindisfarne.

3

Lindisfarne – a place of sanctuary, yet shaped, ominously, like a battle-axe. Serenity here requires constant vigilance; necessitates awareness. Out among the dunes it is all too easy to get lost, as it is to mis-read the tides that come sneaking up through the little gullies to reclaim a temporary precedence.

4

"Do you prize the son of a mare more highly than one of the sons of God?" Aidan had demanded, when a horse King Oswin had given him, he, in turn, had handed on to a footsore beggar. No, these were not men to argue with. *Caveat aut rex.*

5

A warm, moonless night at the end of August. In Bamburgh, by the church he himself had founded, Aidan was dying; dying just as the earth rolled into the path of a seemingly endless storm of meteors – the Perseids; while on a hillside north of Melrose, a young Cuthbert, on watch over the sheepfold, beheld some great soul enter into heaven in a blaze of glory.

6

First in ones and twos, then in their thousands, the puffins are coming home to their burrows on Inner Farne: *fratercula* – little brothers: a clown's face on a monk's robes.

Odd the way the birds of the cliffs and rockface are all either white or black, or black and white: gannet, cormorant, and tern; fulmar and guillemot, kittiwake and gull. And all so raucous of voice – perhaps to compete with the winds and the waves. With one exception: the eider – Cuddy's Duck – coo-rooing and snug in the duvet of its own down.

7

Lifelong and devoted friends, yet sharing a desire to live in solitude – one off the coast of Northumbria, the other on an island on Derwent Water – Cuthbert and Herbert, at their last meeting, formed an agreement, in accordance with which, on the 20th of March in the year 687, while living some hundred miles and more apart, they died together. Even their names had rhymed.

8

Twice a day comes a moment when the downstream flow of little coastal rivers stops; comes to a pause; is held back by the inrush of a rising tide, and *the swan's down feather that stands upon the swell, neither way inclines.* Just so, there are times in the heat of a midsummer's afternoon when the world itself seems to need a siesta. Not a leaf moves. No birds sing. Its stillness quietly redolent of meadowsweet and may.

9

Terrible were the portents – fiery dragons flying in the air. Nor was it thought such an inroad from the sea could be made. The harrying of the heathen. Like wolves they tore and slaughtered; plundered; trampled the holy places with their polluted feet. The Church of Saint Cuthbert they spattered with the blood of priests. Some they slew. Some they took away in fetters. Some they drowned in the sea.

10

What could, only a month or so past, have been taken for a finished painting, today looks, when all the leaves have fallen from the trees, little more than a scribbled outline sketch; and yet, with all the fripperies of spring and autumn's ostentations done and dusted, it could perhaps be said that winter trees are the tree itself, but only if the changes were all over, and no darker days were waiting still to come.

11

For seven years, seven men, to keep out of harm's way, trundled about with the coffin, the Gospels and the relics: Norham, Elsdon, Beltingham, Old Haydon and Selkeld; north to Carlisle; then south again, crossing the sands to Aldingham and Kirkby-in-Furness, abhorring not Millom and Workington. ("Ireland?" "No, no way!") So back once more over the Pennines: Hexham, Chester-le-Street, Ripon, York…

"In Heaven's name, where are we now? This thing's stuck; won't budge!"

"Young maid here says it's called Dunholme."

"Durholme? Well, it'll have to do."

12

Two heads may be better than one, but not, one would have thought, in a coffin. So, when Cuthbert's tomb was opened, King Oswald's was reverently removed, leaving the bishop – his body incorruptible and with the odour of sanctity still sweet about him – to have it all to himself again. Surely the very least any body could ask for.

13

From Lindisfarne to Hobthrush he went and from Hobthrush to Inner Farne; not so much to get away from the world as from those who came between him and the world.

No wind. The snowflakes fall so slowly they seem determined not to land.

This day will not come again.

14

And in Jarrow, Bede wrote: *Not only did the creatures of the air minister to the venerable man, but so too did sea animals and indeed the sea itself.*

Durham now hosts them both: Bede in state in the Galilee Chapel, while the black marble behind the High Altar bears the single name *CUTHBERTUS*. Cuthbert. What more need be said?

THINGS BEING VARIOUS

1

Searching for a resemblance
between the things we can see:

> how the colour blue
> seems to float and hover
> over the flowers of the sea-holly;
> an aspect rather than a quality

and those which we cannot:

> that shiver
> of a morning
> which tells us
> autumn has come

occasions some adjustment to reality.

Memory believes before knowing remembers.

2

Even with the east wind
and the snow excluded,
it was ghostly cold
walking through the woods
this morning; each branch
as velvet as a young deer's
horn, the hoar frost
had so textured them.
Dry leaves veined and brittle,
crackled underfoot, and one
little brown bird,
constantly ahead of me,
was looking for something.

3

Day three and the Voice said:

> Let there be a process
> to be known as photosynthesis,
> whereby the pigment chlorophyll
> by means of the radiant heat of the sun
> will combine with carbon dioxide
> to produce sugar in the form of glucose
> at the same time giving off oxygen;

and the Green Man said:

> when I open
> my mouth
> I utter leaves.

4

The sun had not yet risen;
a pale moon lingered;
pale as the necks
of young girls on the beach
when they lift their hair
for the heat:

while against the darker
dark of the trees,
fireflies were embroidering,
pin-point, their own,
if lesser starlight.

5

Late January, and the temperature
barely above zero all week; the ground
so impacted a pick-axe would bound
right back at you; yet underneath,
snowdrops are slowly working their way up
and through into the daylight; and soon,
before Candlemas, there'll be hundreds of them
modestly hanging their pale heads as though
what they'd achieved was really no great matter.

6

While once they were allowed
Some flighty bits on the side,

Maps now look to be meaning
At its most monogamous:

No cherubs; no *Here be Lions;*
No galleons tilting in the bay.

Holding an increase in fact
To equal an increase in truth,

They ignore the traveller's need
To tell the lie of the land.

7

Who
in the night
severed
all these babies'

hands
and hid them
palms uppermost
under the

walnut tree?
This morning
there are tiny
fingers

and pudgy little
nailless thumbs
around all its
damp roots.

8

All along the riverside
    willows are exchanging
        the wind's gossip

while from deep
    within the reed beds
        a bittern responds

mournfully to the
    sound of the
        14.23 to Arnside.

9

They stand –

from Calanais
and the Ring of Brodgar
to Castlerigg and Carnac:

megalith, dolmen and henge,
cromlech and cairn,
clamorous in their silence;

like stone dreams
they stand,
like the dreams of stones.

10

Once it had been the colour
    of her parasol that caught his eye:
its lining of the deepest indigo
    calling to mind an Italian night-time sky.

Now the night-time sky above Bellagio
    calls to mind the colour
of her parasol, covering
    the world in deepest indigo.

11

Looking down from the height of the sand dunes
in a failing light, I saw what I took
to be an oil slick further off along the beach,
but binos showed it ot be a flock (no),
a flight (no); a slick – yes, that's it – a slick
of oystercatchers, huddled together,
waiting for the tide to give ground enough
for them to start jabbing and hammering
their way into a flotsam of molluscs.

12

July. High summer. A time to lie back
in the shade and take stock of what others
might be getting up to: squadrons of swifts
ceaselessly screeching around the clock-tower;
a bullfinch commandeering the bird-feeder;
and fat-bottomed bees burrowing into the
freckled throats of this full-peal of foxgloves.

13

Just as nightfall sometimes intensifies
the scent of certain flowers, so at first
the very isolation of the island
deepened the savour of his contentment there;

then, as the years passed, he found himself
becoming a student of waves:
observing the rise of each slow-drawn intake,
how it would coil to a poised menace

before the deliberate topple-over and roll,
that whiter-than-ever-snowfall spillage
and rush which rattled the pebbles and grey
stones around his veined and scrawny feet.

14

A low, lingering mist
outlined every twist
and stretch of the river
until well into mid-morning,
when a breath of wind
and some warmth
in the sun unveiled
a flicker of water-lights;
and we could make out
how at the downstream edge
of the weir, the water looked
set to turn around
and climb back up over it.

15

A mist of spores
blowing into the dead
face of a felled birch
as it dries and splits

blossoms as
orange freckles
and fine green hair;
or else garish

fly agaric
blazing out of the mulch
where woodlice huddle
among crumpled ears

and shaggy parasols:
rampant in illusion,
this earth sucks
at its own insane root.

16

You know how,
so very slowly,
snow falls
when there is no wind?
Well, so it is now
with these autumn leaves,
drifting and floating;
seeming to savour
their brief moments
of independence,
and loth to add
to the vast plethora
of the outnumbering dead.

17

Though he leant right out over the rim of the well,
the water was too far down for him to see.

"Time," you realise, someone remarked
inside his head, "is only the rate

at which the past decays." And so
he let slip slowly through his fingers

the one or two choice memories he chanced
to have about him, then stood listening,

attentatively, for their depleted echo.